WWE SURVIVOR SERIES®

SLAM BY SLAM

CRAIG TELLO

SCHOLASTIC

Published by Tangerine Press,
an imprint of Scholastic Inc.,
557 Broadway, New York, NY 10012

an imprint of
SCHOLASTIC
www.scholastic.com

WWE Survivor Series Slam by Slam
is produced by becker&mayer! LLC
11120 NE 33rd Place, Suite 101
Bellevue, WA 98004
www.beckermayer.com

If you have questions or comments about this product,
please visit www.beckermayer.com/customerservice
and click on Customer Service Request Form.

Author: Craig Tello
Editor: Dana Youlin
Production coordinator: Jennifer Marx
Photo researcher: Emily Zach
Designer: Sam Dawson

392392
Printed in Jefferson City, MO USA
10 9 8 7 6 5 4 3 2 1
ISBN: 9780545709668
13661

SURVIVOR SERIES

SLAM BY SLAM

For almost three decades, WWE's finest competitors have strived to survive in the annual *Survivor Series*. The WWE has hosted some of the fiercest, most competitive and unforgettable collisions of the ring's top rivals. Plus, many of sports-entertainment's greatest Superstars made their debuts there. Though the extravaganza and the competitors have evolved over the years, *Survivor Series* has always been a battleground that has shaped the course of WWE's epic history.

THE MATCHUPS

2009:
TEAM KOFI VS. TEAM ORTON

THE HISTORY

"The Viper" Randy Orton used 2009 to establish his legacy. Not only did he recruit successful second-generation Superstars Cody Rhodes and Ted DiBiase to his side, he also won the Royal Rumble. Plus he competed in the main event of WrestleMania XXV and captured the WWE Championship in late April. Orton held the title for three separate reigns throughout the year. He became nastier than ever when he lost the prize to John Cena in October. But an angry Orton made a mistake in thinking he could bully Kofi Kingston.

TEAM KOFI

KOFI KINGSTON (CAPTAIN)
MVP
Mark Henry
Christian
R-Truth

TEAM ORTON

RANDY ORTON (CAPTAIN)
Cody Rhodes
Ted DiBiase
CM Punk
William Regal

FACT

All three fathers of Randy Orton, Cody Rhodes, and Ted DiBiase are WWE Hall of Famers ("Cowboy" Bob Orton, Dusty Rhodes, and The Million Dollar Man).

The rising star fought against The Viper and even destroyed a special car given to Randy Orton. WWE fans will never forget how Kingston used a crowbar and bright orange paint to "remodel" Randy's vehicle. Things got more intense on *Raw* just days before Kingston and Orton captained teams at *Survivor Series*. Orton tried to punt WWE Hall of Famer "Rowdy" Roddy Piper during a rare appearance, but Kofi came to the rescue. He fought The Viper through the crowd and delivered an incredible Boom Drop from the stands! This was a different side of Kofi. He led his Boom Squad into *Survivor Series* to combat Orton's impressive legacy head-on.

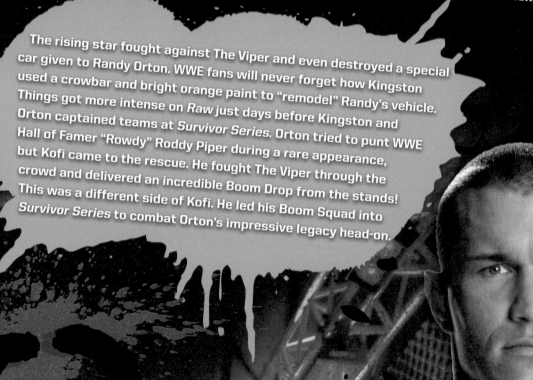

KOFI KINGSTON

STRENGTH

ENDURANCE

MVP

STRENGTH

ENDURANCE

MARK HENRY

STRENGTH

ENDURANCE

CHRISTIAN

STRENGTH

ENDURANCE

R-TRUTH

STRENGTH

ENDURANCE

0 1 2 3 4 5 6 7 8 9 10

THE BATTLE FOR SURVIVAL

Team Kofi had a size, power, and speed advantage. Team Orton had plenty of skill and cunning to compete. The Viper's crew quickly eliminated their largest opponent, Mark Henry, with an illegal team effort and thunderous RKO. They used the same tactics on R-Truth, who fell to CM Punk's Go To Sleep maneuver.

The odds were evened when Christian pinned Ted DiBiase and MVP eliminated William Regal. Next, Cody Rhodes removed MVP from the equation with a Cross Rhodes. But Cody didn't last long—he fell to Christian's Killswitch. Moments later, Christian was hit by a lightning-quick RKO and was pinned by Orton.

TEAM KOFI

It was up to Kingston to collide with his former tag-team partner, CM Punk, and The Viper. Kofi held his own against Punk while Orton circled around the ring, watching the action unfold. Kingston focused on Punk but still kept his eyes on Orton.

Kofi's strategy worked. Almost immediately after pinning Punk with a rollup, Kingston sprang into action as Orton charged him. The Viper ran right into Trouble in Paradise! The kick was enough to stun Orton, and within six seconds Kofi Kingston had pinned two former World Champions to become the sole survivor.

THE STATS

RANDY ORTON
STRENGTH
ENDURANCE

CODY RHODES
STRENGTH
ENDURANCE

TED DIBIASE
STRENGTH
ENDURANCE

CM PUNK
STRENGTH
ENDURANCE

WILLIAM REGAL
STRENGTH
ENDURANCE

10 9 8 7 6 5 4 3 2 1 0

TEAM ORTON

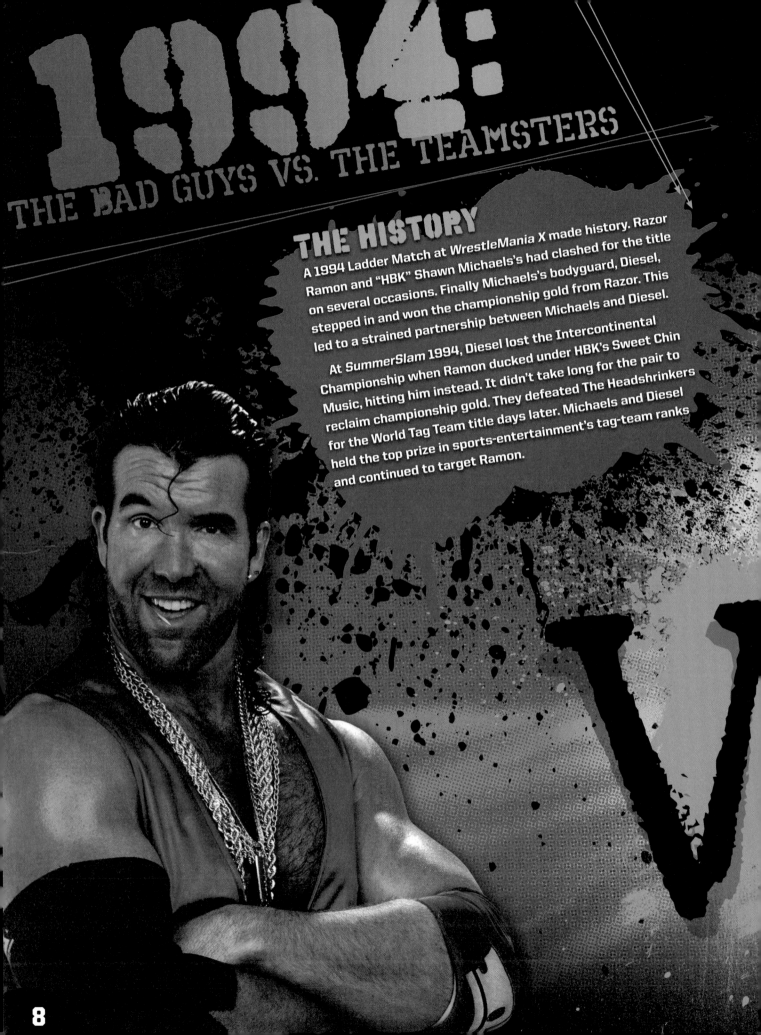

1994:
THE BAD GUYS VS. THE TEAMSTERS

THE HISTORY

A 1994 Ladder Match at WrestleMania X made history. Razor Ramon and "HBK" Shawn Michaels's had clashed for the title on several occasions. Finally Michaels's bodyguard, Diesel, stepped in and won the championship gold from Razor. This led to a strained partnership between Michaels and Diesel.

At SummerSlam 1994, Diesel lost the Intercontinental Championship when Ramon ducked under HBK's Sweet Chin Music, hitting him instead. It didn't take long for the pair to reclaim championship gold. They defeated The Headshrinkers for the World Tag Team title days later. Michaels and Diesel held the top prize in sports-entertainment's tag-team ranks and continued to target Ramon.

THE BAD GUYS

RAZOR RAMON (CAPTAIN)
1-2-3 Kid
British Bulldog
Headshrinker Sione
Headshrinker Fatu

THE TEAMSTERS

SHAWN MICHAELS (CO-CAPTAIN)
DIESEL (CO-CAPTAIN)
Owen Hart
Jim Neidhart
Jeff Jarrett

FACT

Diesel single-handedly eliminated three opponents in this match in just 1 minute, 42 seconds.

Razor rallied The Bad Guys, including his best friend, the 1-2-3 Kid, plus The Headshrinkers and British Bulldog. The Teamsters (co-captains Diesel and Michaels) included another former Intercontinental Champion, Jeff Jarrett, and Bulldog's Hart Family enemies, Jim "The Anvil" Neidhart and Owen Hart.

Tensions were high—especially among The Teamsters themselves. With HBK's ego starting to wear on Diesel's patience, all eyes were on this match to see who would survive.

S.

RAZOR RAMON

STRENGTH

ENDURANCE

1-2-3 KID

STRENGTH

ENDURANCE

BRITISH BULLDOG

STRENGTH

ENDURANCE

HEADSHRINKER SIONE

STRENGTH

ENDURANCE

HEADSHRINKER FATU

STRENGTH

ENDURANCE

0 1 2 3 4 5 6 7 8 9 10

THE BATTLE FOR SURVIVAL

Minutes went by as The Bad Guys collided with The Teamsters without either squad taking the advantage—that is, until Diesel tagged in. The big man instantly brought down Headshrinker Fatu, then flattened the 1-2-3 Kid, and finally crushed Fatu's partner, Sione. Diesel's impressive Jackknife Powerbomb took them all out in less than two minutes. The British Bulldog was eliminated moments later after a boot from Diesel knocked him outside, where he was attacked by rival team members.

Razor Ramon was outnumbered 5-to-1 against the Teamsters. He bravely battled Diesel head-on, while HBK barked orders from the side. When Diesel finally got Ramon where he wanted him, Michaels demanded to be tagged in for the winning pinfall, but he pressed his luck just a bit too far. HBK forced Diesel to hold Razor up for easily executed Sweet Chin Music and missed, hitting his partner instead!

THE BAD GUYS

SHAWN MICHAELS

STRENGTH

ENDURANCE

DIESEL

STRENGTH

ENDURANCE

OWEN HART

STRENGTH

ENDURANCE

JIM NEIDHART

STRENGTH

ENDURANCE

JEFF JARRETT

STRENGTH

ENDURANCE

10 9 8 7 6 5 4 3 2 1 0

FACT

Diesel was the first Superstar in WWE to win the Intercontinental, World Tag Team, and WWE Championships all in the same year.

For a third time, Diesel was struck by Michaels's kick and was fed up. The angry giant marched toward HBK, who fled toward the locker room, followed by Diesel and the rest of The Teamsters. Diesel blasted each of them for their attempts to intervene. Amid the chaos, all five team members were eliminated, giving the recovering Razor Ramon the win as sole survivor.

THE TEAMSTERS

2008!

JOHN CENA VS. WORLD HEAVYWEIGHT CHAMPION CHRIS JERICHO

THE HISTORY

John Cena made a leap of faith at SummerSlam 2008. In a grueling clash with Batista, the Cenation leader leapt from the top rope and ended up in a mid-air Batista Bomb. The impact left Cena with a herniated disc in his neck that required surgery and three months away from the ring.

Meanwhile a scheming "Y2J" Chris Jericho snuck his way into the running for the World Heavyweight Title. He took an open spot in the first-ever Championship Scramble and won. Cena's rival Batista took the championship from Jericho at Cyber Sunday.

JOHN CENA
CHRIS JERICHO

FACT

John Cena had three WWE Championship reigns before claiming his first World Heavyweight at *Survivor Series* 2008.

Y2J took the prize from Batista inside a steel cage on *Raw's* 800th episode celebration. The scheming Superstar added the World Heavyweight Championship to his wardrobe of suits and ties, and no challenger could top Jericho's combination of in-ring ability and underhandedness.

As *Survivor Series* quickly approached, all eyes in the WWE Universe were on Cena. The gladiator from West Newbury, Massachusetts was set to make his return, and there was no better setting than *Survivor Series*. Cena was ready for a fight and the multiple World Champion's first match back in WWE was going to be against none other than Chris Jericho.

JOHN CENA

STRENGTH

|||||||||||||||||||||||||||||||||||||||||||||

ENDURANCE

|||||||||||||||||||||||||||||||||||||||||

0 1 2 3 4 5 6 7 8 9 10

THE BATTLE FOR SURVIVAL

There was much speculation about John Cena's condition after surgery. Many wondered whether or not the Cenation leader had come back too soon, especially against a wicked opponent like Chris Jericho. Jericho would do absolutely anything to keep the World Heavyweight around his waist.

This is why Jericho immediately targeted Cena's neck at the start of the match. He unleashed double-arm DDTs, a Full Nelson submission hold, and even a modified Walls of Jericho that directly affected Cena's recently repaired neck. But Cena was resilient and fought back, displaying his signature strength and courage. He even regained the confidence to perform the move that had injured him months earlier: the top-rope legdrop.

FACT

Five years after beating Chris Jericho, John Cena successfully defended the same World Heavyweight Title in his third reign against Alberto Del Rio at Survivor Series 2013.

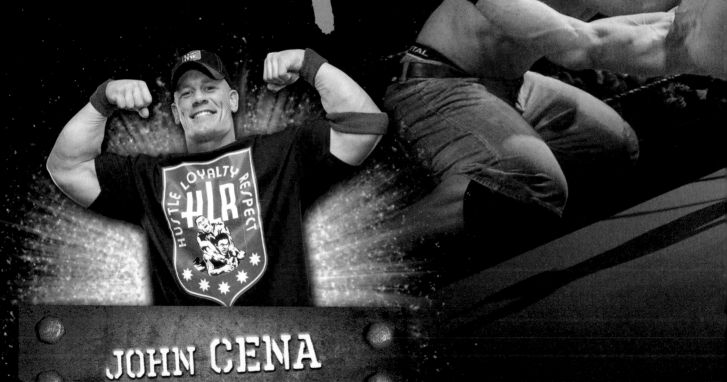

JOHN CENA

CHRIS JERICHO

STRENGTH

|||||||||||||||||||||||||||||||||

ENDURANCE

|||||||||||||||||||||||||||||||

10 9 8 7 6 5 4 3 2 1 0

Cena brought on the Attitude Adjustment and Jericho used the Code Breaker, but neither man fell. Finally, as Jericho attempted an inside cradle, Cena reversed and used his impressive power to lift the champion and deliver a massive Attitude Adjustment. This second dose of Cena's celebrated move was enough to keep Jericho down for the three-count. The leader of the Cenation triumphantly won the first World Heavyweight Championship of his career.

CHRIS JERICHO

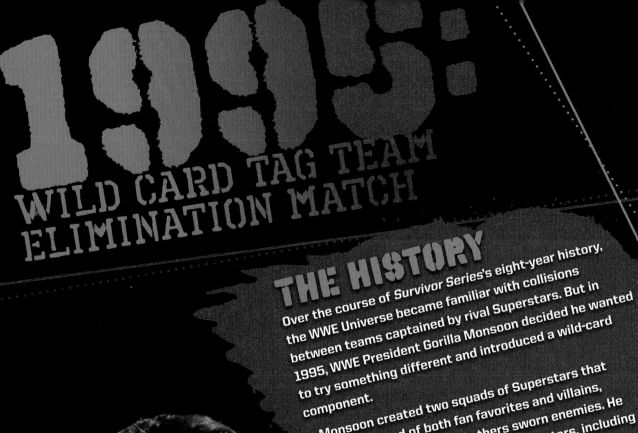

1990s:
WILD CARD TAG TEAM ELIMINATION MATCH

THE HISTORY

Over the course of Survivor Series's eight-year history, the WWE Universe became familiar with collisions between teams captained by rival Superstars. But in 1995, WWE President Gorilla Monsoon decided he wanted to try something different and introduced a wild-card component.

Monsoon created two squads of Superstars that were composed of both fan favorites and villains, some tag teammates and others sworn enemies. He set up unexpected groupings of Superstars, including Intercontinental Champion Razor Ramon alongside captain Yokozuna and Owen Hart, plus the top contender for Razor's title, Dean Douglas. Their opposition was Team Michaels, with HBK, his former bodyguard-turned-enemy Sid, British Bulldog, and newcomer Ahmed Johnson.

THE MICHAELS

SHAWN MICHAELS (CAPTAIN)

Ahmed Johnson

British Bulldog

Sycho Sid

THE YOKOZUNA

YOKOZUNA (CO-CAPTAIN)

RAZOR RAMON (CO-CAPTAIN)

Owen Hart

Dean Douglas

FACT

Survivor Series 1995 was Ahmed Johnson's first time in action on pay-per-view.

Both teams headed into *Survivor Series* uncertain about whether they could trust their partners enough to win (and keep their past issues from exploding at ringside).

A month earlier, Ramon had beaten Douglas for the Intercontinental Championship, stirring bad blood between the two. Even manager Jim Cornette found himself torn between three members of his camp who had been placed on opposing teams. And Sid ... he was just plain Sycho.

THE BATTLE FOR SURVIVAL

SHAWN MICHAELS

STRENGTH

|||||||||||||||||||||||||||||||||||||||||||

ENDURANCE

||||||||||||||||||||||||||||||||||||||||||||

AHMED JOHNSON

STRENGTH

|||||||||||||||||||||||||||||||||||||||||

ENDURANCE

|||||||||||||||||||||||||||||||||||

BRITISH BULLDOG

STRENGTH

|||||||||||||||||||||||||||||||||||||

ENDURANCE

||||||||||||||||||||||||||||||||||

SYCHO SID

STRENGTH

||||||||||||||||||||||||||||||||||||||||

ENDURANCE

||||||||||||||||||||||||||||||||||||||

0 1 2 3 4 5 6 7 8 9 10

The teammates distrusted one another right up to the minutes before the Wild-Card Tag Team Elimination Match. This made for an unpredictable clash of eight top Superstars. It appeared that Shawn Michaels found common ground among his squad and formed an alliance with powerful rookie Ahmed Johnson. But on Team Yokozuna, the only fan favorite was Razor Ramon, and he was surrounded by enemies. It didn't help that Ramon's former friend, 1-2-3 Kid, had won his *Survivor Series* match by cheating earlier in the night.

Ramon had little patience for Dean Douglas from the beginning and when things got intense, Douglas paid for it. After Ramon struck Douglas, he was eliminated. Team Michaels also suffered from miscommunication as Michaels delivered Sweet Chin Music to his own partner, Sid. Ramon capitalized on this and eliminated Sid. Next, Johnson used his fierce Pearl River Plunge to put away Owen Hart.

FACT

Shawn Michaels and Razor Ramon have faced off in two epic Ladder Matches for the Intercontinental. They each won one match.

TEAM MICHAELS

Suddenly, Sid returned with 1-2-3 Kid to get Razor's attention, leading to Ramon's elimination at the hands of the Bulldog. Even the mighty and massive former WWE Champion Yokozuna couldn't overcome a 3-on-1 disadvantage. The 500-pound sumo star was defeated after Sweet Chin Music from HBK and a thunderous splash by Johnson. Team Michaels was victorious.

MOVE: SWEET CHIN MUSIC

SMACK!

RAZOR RAMON
STRENGTH

ENDURANCE

YOKOZUNA
STRENGTH

ENDURANCE

OWEN HART
STRENGTH

ENDURANCE

DEAN DOUGLAS
STRENGTH

ENDURANCE

10 9 8 7 6 5 4 3 2 1 0

TEAM YOKOZUNA & RAMON

THE HISTORY

"The Deadman" Undertaker took aim at The Immortal Hulk Hogan and the WWE Championship in the fall of 1991. For 12 months, the sinister Deadman slowly gripped WWE with his grey gloves, devastating countless competitors and proving to be unstoppable. The only way to counter fear is to have courage—and no other Superstar in WWE at the time was as courageous as Hulk Hogan.

During the rise of Deadman, another Superstar emerged in the spotlight: "Nature Boy" Ric Flair. The golden boy of WCW stole the world's attention by claiming that he was the undisputed champion of the ring. And he had a large, golden World Heavyweight Championship to prove it.

HULK HOGAN
UNDERTAKER

FACT

Hulk Hogan's match with Undertaker was labeled "The Gravest Challenge."

Flair showed off his prize despite WWE's recognized champion, Hogan. This gave Hogan not just one but two major enemies in late '91.

On the set of The Funeral Parlor—the talk show for Paul Bearer and the evil Undertaker—The Deadman and Flair caught Hogan by surprise and attacked the champion. Just before Survivor Series, it appeared that Hulk Hogan had finally met his "Gravest Challenge."

HULK HOGAN

STRENGTH

||||||||||||||||||||||||||||||||||

ENDURANCE

||||||||||||||||||||||||||||||||

0 1 2 3 4 5 6 7 8 9 10

FACT

Undertaker lost the WWE Championship to Hulk Hogan less than a week after Survivor Series at This Tuesday in Texas.

HULK HOGAN

THE BATTLE FOR SURVIVAL

Hogan had overcome his share of monsters, from Earthquake to Andre the Giant. But none had the supernatural power of Undertaker. That didn't stop Hulk from running wild on a casket sitting at ringside. Hogan refused to be intimidated by The Deadman.

Inside the ring, Hulk bravely fought Undertaker, but Hogan struggled to take the 7-footer off his feet. The only thing more awe-inspiring than Undertaker's defense was his offense, which weakened and hurt Hogan throughout the contest. It seemed the WWE Universe would see the end of The Immortal One. But, proving he perhaps was Immortal, Hogan recovered from Undertaker's Tombstone and unleashed his infamous punches, bringing his challenger to one knee.

UNDERTAKER

STRENGTH

ENDURANCE

10 9 8 7 6 5 4 3 2 1 0

Then, Nature Boy stormed to the ring and received a furious fist from Hogan that knocked Flair to the floor. The champion prepared to deliver his signature legdrop to the fallen Deadman, but Paul Bearer grabbed Hogan's ankle long enough for Undertaker to recover. Hulk walked right into his enemy's arms and a second Tombstone. He came down on a steel chair placed in the ring by Flair. Three counts later, Undertaker was crowned the new WWE Champion, setting WWE on a journey into darkness.

UNDERTAKER

2006:
TEAM DX VS. TEAM RATED-RKO

THE HISTORY

In late 2006, the original DX members, Triple H and Shawn Michaels, reformed their group and turned WWE upside down. The pair targeted the McMahons, painted WWE Headquarters with their lime green logo, and defied every rule along the way. But things got serious fast, thanks to Edge.

Edge convinced Randy Orton that DX was a threat. He reminded Orton of his history with Triple H and blamed him for Orton's dip in successes. Together, they vowed to destroy the legacy of DX. They formed "Rated-RKO" and defeated Triple H and HBK at Cyber Sunday, with help from scheming referee Eric Bischoff.

TEAM DX
TRIPLE H (CO-CAPTAIN)
SHAWN MICHAELS (CO-CAPTAIN)
CM Punk
Jeff Hardy
Matt Hardy

TEAM RATED-RKO
EDGE (CO-CAPTAIN)
RANDY ORTON (CO-CAPTAIN)
Johnny Nitro
Mike Knox
Gregory Helms

The bad blood continued to boil as Edge and Orton viciously punished World Tag Team Champions Ric Flair and Roddy Piper, taking the titles. The brutality of their win made it much more personal for Triple H and Michaels. They assembled an all-star team that included top ECW competitor CM Punk, plus the recently reunited Hardys. Rated-RKO responded by recruiting Jeff Hardy's archrival and Intercontinental Champion Johnny Nitro, plus Mike Knox and Gregory Helms. With the battle lines drawn, there was only one question left for either team: Are you ready?

FACT

More than a decade before their reunion, Shawn Michaels and Triple H originally formed D-Generation X in late 1997.

THE STATS

TRIPLE H
STRENGTH

||||||||||||||||||||||

ENDURANCE

||||||||||||||||||||||

SHAWN MICHAELS
STRENGTH

||||||||||||||||||||||

ENDURANCE

||||||||||||||||||||||

CM PUNK
STRENGTH

||||||||||||||||||||||

ENDURANCE

||||||||||||||||||||||

JEFF HARDY
STRENGTH

||||||||||||||||||||||

ENDURANCE

||||||||||||||||||||||

MATT HARDY
STRENGTH

||||||||||||||||||||||

ENDURANCE

||||||||||||||||||||||

0 1 2 3 4 5 6 7 8 9 10

THE BATTLE FOR SURVIVAL

Live in Philadelphia, Team DX had the crowd behind them. This gave them enough momentum for what would end up being a shutout of their rivals.

Team Rated-RKO's Mike Knox received Sweet Chin Music from Michaels and was the first eliminated. The next to fall was the crafty Intercontinental Champion, Johnny Nitro. He tapped out to CM Punk's Anaconda Vise. Things got worse for Edge and Randy Orton when Cruiserweight Champion Gregory Helms fell to a combo Twist of Fate and Swanton Bomb by the Hardys.

TEAM DX

26

The most wicked members of Team Rated-RKO, Flair and Piper, were left to battle the full Team DX. Instead of fighting, the cowardly duo tried to escape their fate and exit to the locker room. This failed as Jeff and Matt Hardy chased them down. Back in the ring, Edge tasted Sweet Chin Music and was eliminated. Next, Orton—who tried to run again—met Sweet Chin Music, followed by a Pedigree. A three-count later, all five members of Team DX had survived and executed a clean sweep of their enemies.

EDGE
STRENGTH

ENDURANCE

RANDY ORTON
STRENGTH

ENDURANCE

JOHNNY NITRO
STRENGTH

ENDURANCE

MIKE KNOX
STRENGTH

ENDURANCE

GREGORY HELMS
STRENGTH

ENDURANCE

10 9 8 7 6 5 4 3 2 1 0

FACT

WWE Hall of Famer Lita competed in her final match at *Survivor Series 2006*, where she lost the Women's Title to Mickie James.

TEAM RATED-RKO

1995:
THE DARKSIDE VS. THE ROYALS

THE HISTORY

A battle for the throne at King of the Ring 1995 started a half-year rivalry between Undertaker and the massive King Mabel. In pursuit of the crown, Mabel faced off against Undertaker during the single-night tournament. Mabel seized the title of "King" with the help of The Deadman's enemy Kama.

Months later, Undertaker challenged Mabel's kingdom and suffered the wrath of his majesty. The Deadman was battered with avalanche splashes and multiple legdrops. Very few individuals in the history of sports-entertainment had ever manhandled Undertaker in such a way, proving King Mabel's power.

THE DARKSIDE
UNDERTAKER (CAPTAIN)
Savio Vega

Henry O. Godwinn

Fatu

THE ROYALS
KING MABEL (CAPTAIN)
Jerry Lawler

Hunter Hearst-Helmsley

Isaac Yankem

FACT

An undefeated Hunter Hearst-Helmsley made his first Survivor Series appearance in 1995. He would later drop his snobby handle in place of the name he goes by today: Triple H.

More than a month later, *Survivor Series 1995* was set to host the return of The Deadman. He and his tag team partners Savio Vega, Henry O. Godwinn, and Fatu formed The Darkside. They would combat The Royals, captained by King Mabel with Jerry "The King" Lawler, his demented dentist Isaac Yankem, and Hunter Hearst-Helmsley. Rumors of a different and changed Undertaker added to the chill in the air heading into *Survivor Series*. It became very clear that King Mabel's reign in WWE was about to be confronted by the cold hands of justice.

UNDERTAKER

STRENGTH

ENDURANCE

SAVIO VEGA

STRENGTH

ENDURANCE

HENRY O. GODWINN

STRENGTH

ENDURANCE

FATU

STRENGTH

ENDURANCE

0 1 2 3 4 5 6 7 8 9 10

THE BATTLE FOR SURVIVAL

King Mabel was carried in a throne down the aisle to the ring. His impressive entrance was quickly overcome by the shadow of darkness—the arrival of Undertaker. There was only one thing more chilling than the returning Superstar's emergence: the revelation of his frightening face protector.

From beneath a creepy mask covering his injuries, The Deadman stared down his four foes, then began to dominate them, one by one. The first victim was Jerry Lawler, whose team avoided his tags because they were afraid of The Deadman. Isaac Yankem suffered a Tombstone moments later. Next, Hunter Hearst-Helmsley tried to flee, only to be threatened by the contents of Henry Godwinn's slop bucket. As Helmsley backed up he was grabbed by Undertaker and chokeslammed.

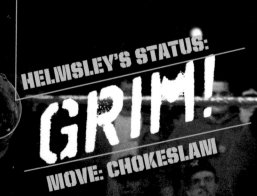

HELMSLEY'S STATUS:

GRIM!

MOVE: CHOKESLAM

THE DARKSIDE

The final Royal was Undertaker's biggest target. King Mabel traded blows with The Deadman and got the upper hand, again leveling him with the same face-crushing legdrop that put The Deadman out of commission. But Undertaker rose up, powered by vengeance and his supernatural abilities. The dancing Mabel was spooked by his resilient rival and retreated in fear, leaving his aide, Sir Mo, to feel The Deadman's wrath instead. The Darkside prevailed with all four members surviving, but Undertaker had yet to fully exact his revenge on King Mabel.

KING MABEL

STRENGTH
|||||||||||||||||||||

ENDURANCE
|||||||||||||||||||||

JERRY LAWLER

STRENGTH
|||||||||||||||||||

ENDURANCE
|||||||||||||||||

HUNTER HEARST-HELMSLEY

STRENGTH
|||||||||||||||||||

ENDURANCE
|||||||||||||||||||||

ISAAC YANKEM

STRENGTH
|||||||||||||||||||||

ENDURANCE
|||||||||||||||||||

10 9 8 7 6 5 4 3 2 1 0

FACT

At 568 pounds (1,250 kg), it took four men to carry King Mabel to the ring on his royal platform.

THE ROYALS

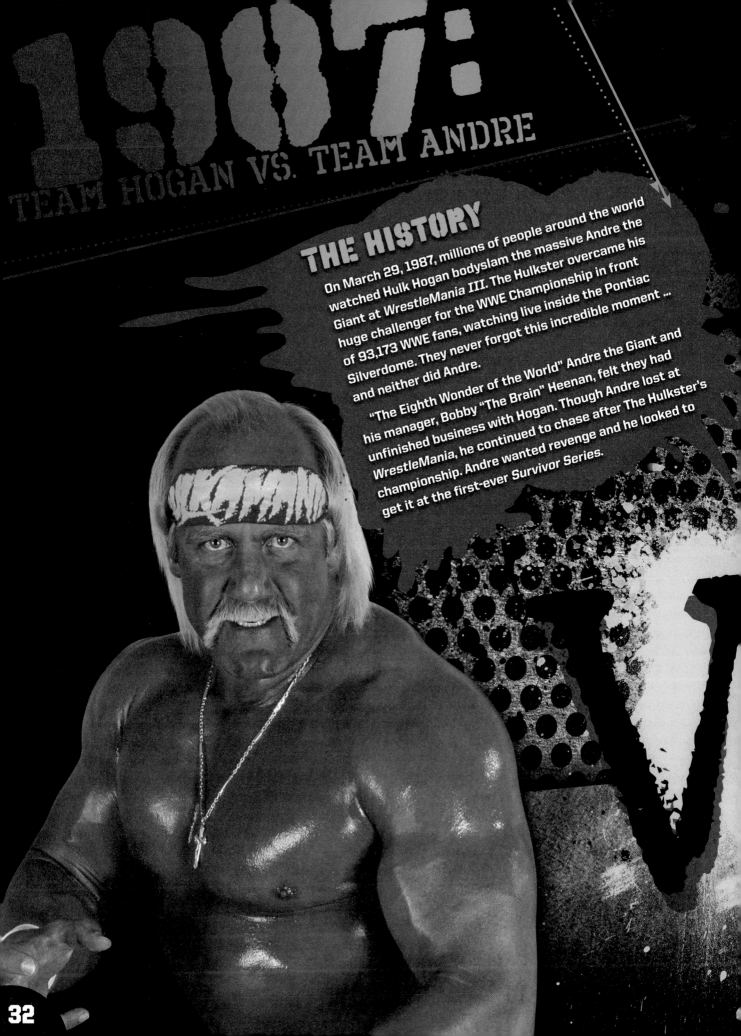

1987:
TEAM HOGAN VS. TEAM ANDRE

THE HISTORY

On March 29, 1987, millions of people around the world watched Hulk Hogan bodyslam the massive Andre the Giant at WrestleMania III. The Hulkster overcame his huge challenger for the WWE Championship in front of 93,173 WWE fans, watching live inside the Pontiac Silverdome. They never forgot this incredible moment ... and neither did Andre.

"The Eighth Wonder of the World" Andre the Giant and his manager, Bobby "The Brain" Heenan, felt they had unfinished business with Hogan. Though Andre lost at WrestleMania, he continued to chase after The Hulkster's championship. Andre wanted revenge and he looked to get it at the first-ever Survivor Series.

TEAM HOGAN

HULK HOGAN (CAPTAIN)

Paul Orndorff

Bam Bam Bigelow

Ken Patera

Don Muraco

TEAM ANDRE

ANDRE THE GIANT (CAPTAIN)

King Kong Bundy

"Ravishing" Rick Rude

One Man Gang

Butch Reed

The five members of Team Andre weighed a combined 1,943 pounds (4,275 kg), outweighing Team Hogan by about 500 pounds (1,100 kg)!

The Giant looked to WWE's biggest villains—"Ravishing" Rick Rude, King Kong Bundy, Butch Reed, and The One Man Gang—to round out his squad. Hulk Hogan didn't have to look too far to find allies. The Hulkster assembled a team that included Bam Bam Bigelow, Don Muraco, Paul Orndorff, and Ken Patera. Months after the titanic WrestleMania clash, Team Andre and Team Hogan would continue one of the greatest rivalries in sports-entertainment history.

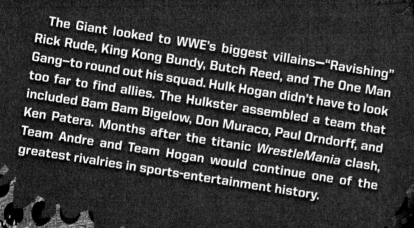

HULK HOGAN
STRENGTH

ENDURANCE

PAUL ORNDORFF
STRENGTH

ENDURANCE

BAM BAM BIGELOW
STRENGTH

ENDURANCE

KEN PATERA
STRENGTH

ENDURANCE

DON MURACO
STRENGTH

ENDURANCE

0 1 2 3 4 5 6 7 8 9 10

THE BATTLE FOR SURVIVAL

Team Andre marched into the first-ever Survivor Series intent on crushing Team Hogan. The Hulkster's opposition was huge, but not unbeatable, proven with the elimination of Butch Reed.

What Hogan's team lacked in weight, they made up for in strength. Still, not even powerhouse Ken Patera could withstand the immense One Man Gang. Next, Orndorff, Rick Rude, and Don Muraco were each eliminated. Then came the biggest blow to The Hulkster's crew. Hogan re-created his impressive WrestleMania III feat by slamming his rival behemoths Gang and Bundy. But Team Andre's underhanded tactics got the best of the WWE Champion. He ended up being counted out and eliminated from the match moments later. Bigelow was the final member of Team Hogan. He used his uncanny speed to overcome and pin two of three remaining enemies, but the exhausted Bam Bam fell to The Eighth Wonder of the World's brute force.

The match was over, and the long-awaited confrontation between Andre and Hogan appeared as if it would never happen. Until The Hulkster reemerged. As Andre celebrated, Hogan ambushed him, using the WWE Championship to stun his foe. The giant may have won the battle, but it was The Hulkster who won the war.

TEAM HOGAN

ANDRE THE GIANT
STRENGTH

ENDURANCE

KING KONG BUNDY
STRENGTH

ENDURANCE

"RAVISHING" RICK RUDE
STRENGTH

ENDURANCE

ONE MAN GANG
STRENGTH

ENDURANCE

BUTCH REED
STRENGTH

ENDURANCE

10 9 8 7 6 5 4 3 2 1 0

FACT

A year earlier at WrestleMania II, Hulk Hogan defeated King Kong Bundy in the first steel-cage match to ever take place at The Show of Shows.

TEAM ANDRE

1996:
UNDERTAKER VS. MANKIND

THE HISTORY

The Undertaker had finally met his match when Mankind arrived in WWE in 1996. This wasn't just because the masked madman was a twisted maniac. Mankind had lured Undertaker's longtime manager, Paul Bearer, into betraying The Deadman.

The WWE Universe was stunned at SummerSlam 1996 when Bearer struck Undertaker with his own sacred symbol, the urn. Mankind defeated Undertaker that night in the first Boiler Room Brawl in WWE history and joined forces with Bearer. The Deadman wouldn't be denied vengeance, though. Justice was delivered at In Your House: Mind Games that September, as Undertaker assaulted his enemy. Mankind lost the WWE Championship in a match against champion Shawn Michaels.

UNDERTAKER MANKIND

Next, the rivals squared off at Buried Alive, in a bout as wicked as any other in sports-entertainment history. With the help of The Executioner, Mankind drove The Deadman into a ditch of dirt and covered his entire body in soil, then celebrated on top of the mound. Suddenly, lightning struck, sending Mankind and company from the marked headstone. Undertaker's purple-gloved hand rose from the dirt. Mankind had not seen the last of the iconic Superstar.

UNDERTAKER

STRENGTH

ENDURANCE

0 1 2 3 4 5 6 7 8 9 10

MOVE: TOMBSTONE

SLAM!!!

UNDERTAKER

THE BATTLE FOR SURVIVAL

Undertaker returned from the grave darker than ever before. In all black leather, The Deadman arrived in the *Survivor Series* arena from above, dropping down to the ring with bat-like wings.

Paul Bearer was raised overhead in a small cage to keep him from interfering. The Deadman was fiercer than ever and used a new, more aggressive set of moves to punish Mankind. Undertaker unleashed quick punches and submission holds to combat his rival. The freakish madman fought back, catching Undertaker with the Mandible Claw four separate times. But Undertaker would not stay down. With Bearer screaming instructions at Mankind from above, the undead Superstar captured his enemy in his arms and delivered a Tombstone for the win.

MANKIND

STRENGTH

ENDURANCE

10 9 8 7 6 5 4 3 2 1 0

With that, the cage containing Bearer was lowered, granting Undertaker the chance to get revenge. Suddenly, the hooded Executioners attacked Undertaker. This gave Paul Bearer the opportunity to escape his grim fate while Undertaker fought off his masked enemies. He was triumphant in his return, but Undetaker's war with Paul Bearer and his wicked associates was far from over.

MANKIND

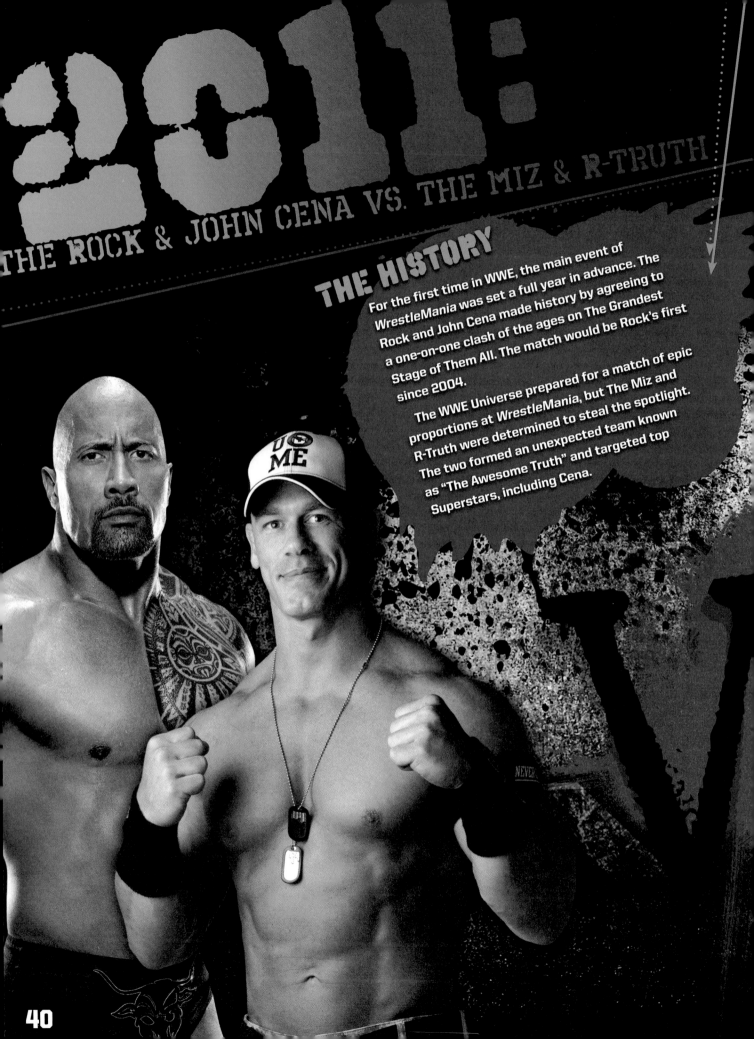

2011:

THE ROCK & JOHN CENA VS. THE MIZ & R-TRUTH

THE HISTORY

For the first time in WWE, the main event of WrestleMania was set a full year in advance. The Rock and John Cena made history by agreeing to a one-on-one clash of the ages on The Grandest Stage of Them All. The match would be Rock's first since 2004.

The WWE Universe prepared for a match of epic proportions at WrestleMania, but The Miz and R-Truth were determined to steal the spotlight. The two formed an unexpected team known as "The Awesome Truth" and targeted top Superstars, including Cena.

JOHN CENA
THE ROCK

THE MIZ
R-TRUTH

It appeared the Cenation leader could not overcome the twosome himself and Raw authority figure John Laurinaitis gave him a choice for *Survivor Series*: Cena could select any partner to face off with Miz and Truth. His pick? "The People's Champion" The Rock.

Cena's choice stunned WWE fans, but it sparked questions about whether The Rock could still compete. Would he still electrify? Could he still lay the smackdown? The world wouldn't have to wait until *WrestleMania* to find out. The People's Champion was coming home to WWE at *Survivor Series*.

FACT

The Rock and John Cena battled for the WWE Title at back-to-back WrestleManias in 2012 (won by Rock) and 2013 (won by Cena).

41

THE STATS

JOHN CENA
STRENGTH

|||||||||||||||||||||||||||||||||||

ENDURANCE

|||||||||||||||||||||||||||||

THE ROCK
STRENGTH

||||||||||||||||||||||||||||||

ENDURANCE

|||||||||||||||||||||||||||||||||

0 1 2 3 4 5 6 7 8 9 10

FACT

There were 2,807 days between The Rock's last match in WWE in 2004 and his return to action at Survivor Series 2011. Both happened in Madison Square Garden.

THE BATTLE FOR SURVIVAL

Fifteen years after The Rock debuted at *Survivor Series* in Madison Square Garden, The People's Champ returned alongside John Cena.

For all the excitement around The Rock's return, there were questions about whether he and Cena could work together as a team. On top of trust issues, The Awesome Truth were in the opposing corner of the ring and vicious as ever. The two worked together to keep Rock out of the match while they focused on weakening Cena with double-teams and underhanded tactics. The Cenation leader fought back with an STF on Miz and an Attitude Adjustment to Truth, but he was too exhausted to gain the upper hand.

Finally, The People's Champ got the tag and unleashed electric blows on his enemies. With Cena taking out R-Truth, The Rock managed to deliver a massive People's Elbow to Miz, pin the former WWE Champion, and earn his team the win.

Afterward, the New York City crowd exploded and welcomed Rock back home to WWE. Rock and Cena stood eye-to-eye in the center of the ring. The titans shared tense words until The People's Champ dropped Cena with a Rock Bottom. Their Road to WrestleMania officially picked up some speed.

ROCK / CENA

THE MIZ

STRENGTH

ENDURANCE

R-TRUTH

STRENGTH

ENDURANCE

10 9 8 7 6 5 4 3 2 1 0

AWESOME TRUTH

1997:
WWE CHAMPION BRET HART VS. SHAWN MICHAELS

THE HISTORY

The WWE Universe still talks about the incredible 60-minute WWE Iron Man Match between Bret Hart and "HBK" Shawn Michaels at WrestleMania XII. That night, two of the most talented Superstars to ever compete made magic for more than an hour. But the clash was just the beginning for Hart and Michaels. The two men shared the most personal rivalry ever seen in sports-entertainment.

BRET HART
SHAWN MICHAELS

A year after WrestleMania XII, Hart captured the WWE Championship for a fifth time by defeating Undertaker at SummerSlam, all thanks to special referee Shawn Michaels! HBK allowed his issues with Bret to get the best of him and lost the title. Michaels wanted it back at Survivor Series 1997.

Though Bret Hart had the support of The Hart Foundation, HBK found a lifelong ally in Triple H. The two formed D-Generation X. Michaels spent months disrespecting WWE officials, Hart, and his native country, Canada. At last, the two entered a match with more at stake than any other bout of their careers.

FACT

Bret Hart and Shawn Michaels battled for The "Hit Man's" WWE Championship five years earlier at Survivor Series 1992.

BRET HART

STRENGTH

ENDURANCE

0 1 2 3 4 5 6 7 8 9 10

THE BATTLE FOR SURVIVAL

With no Hart Foundation or DX at ringside, it was just WWE Champion Bret Hart and European Champion Shawn Michaels at *Survivor Series*—plus 20,000 vocal Canadian WWE fans who sided with the Hart. Personal issues immediately came into play. HBK jumped Bret from behind and started a pre-match fight that crossed through the loud crowd multiple times before the starting bell ever rang.

It took more than a half-dozen officials to try to get the actual match underway, and when they did, Hart pummeled his enemy for much of their match. Instead of his usual technical moves, Hart used powerful fists to weaken his opponent. The punishment continued with an assault on Michaels's legs, including a painful Figure-Four around the ringpost.

HBK pulled the referee into the way of Hart's attack. Now with the advantage, HBK locked in Bret's own Sharpshooter on the WWE Champion! The ref recovered and suddenly called for the bell, as if Hart had submitted to his own hold. The WWE Universe—and Bret himself—were shocked by the scheme. HBK, the referee, and Vince McMahon robbed Hart of the Championship in his final match in WWE. In one of WWE's darkest moments, Michaels quickly fled with the Championship, and a betrayed Bret Hart left WWE for more than a decade.

FACT

On January 4, 2010, Bret Hart returned to WWE and resolved his issues with Shawn Michaels, ending with an emotional hug.

BRET'S STATUS:

SHOCKED

MOVE: SHARPSHOOTER!

BRET HART

SHAWN MICHAELS

STRENGTH

ENDURANCE

10 9 8 7 6 5 4 3 2 1 0

SHAWN MICHAELS

2005:
TEAM RAW VS. TEAM SMACKDOWN

THE HISTORY

You could say the battle between *Raw* and *SmackDown* started the day the WWE roster was split in 2002. For years, both brands competed to be the WWE Universe's favorite. But it got interesting at WWE Homecoming in 2005. That night, top *SmackDown* Superstars were set to compete until *Raw* General Manager Eric Bischoff insulted the competitors and shut out the lights in the arena. This started a war across WWE's rival rosters. Gathered by *SmackDown* GM Theodore Long, World Heavyweight Champion Batista and Rey Mysterio triumphed in different cross-promotional *Raw* vs. *SmackDown* bouts at Taboo Tuesday.

COMBATANTS

TEAM SMACKDOWN

BATISTA (CAPTAIN)

Rey Mysterio
Randy Orton
JBL
Bobby Lashley

TEAM RAW

SHAWN MICHAELS (CAPTAIN)

Kane
Big Show
Carlito
Chris Masters

Detroit's Joe Louis Arena hosted two Survivor Series, both 1991 and 2005.

From there, an embarrassed Bischoff laid down a challenge. He asked Long to select five of his best men to collide against five of *Raw's* best in a Traditional Elimination Tag Team Match at *Survivor Series*. Not only did the so-called "second-rate show" accept, they held their own in SmackDown sneak attacks, *Raw* ambushes, and a rosters-wide brawl between both locker rooms.

The biggest blow came from the massive hands of Big Show and Kane, who double-chokeslammed SmackDown Team Captain Batista through a table days before *Survivor Series*. This left many WWE fans wondering how the SmackDown warriors could possibly win this battle for the ultimate bragging rights.

THE STATS

BATISTA
STRENGTH

ENDURANCE

REY MYSTERIO
STRENGTH

ENDURANCE

RANDY ORTON
STRENGTH

ENDURANCE

JBL
STRENGTH

ENDURANCE

BOBBY LASHLEY
STRENGTH

ENDURANCE

0 1 2 3 4 5 6 7 8 9 10

THE BATTLE FOR SURVIVAL

The *SmackDown* squad of "The Animal" Batista, Rey Mysterio, Randy Orton, JBL, and Bobby Lashley arrived at Detroit's Joe Louis Arena ready to survive against Eric Bischoff's handpicked group of "HBK" Shawn Michaels, Big Show, Kane, Carlito, and Chris Masters.

Powerhouse Lashley was the first to fall, pinned by HBK after suffering an illegal chokeslam from Kane. He paid the price, though, moments later with a 619 from Rey, and a spinebuster by Batista. After being eliminated, Kane got one last shot in on The Animal, with a double-chokeslam. To the shock of WWE fans, within an instant *SmackDown's* captain was pinned, defeated, and removed from the match.

The *SmackDown* team rallied back from their major loss and used the signature move of every remaining member to beat the mammoth Big Show. It took two Clotheslines from Hell, a 619, an RKO, and a seated senton to drop him. Team *SmackDown* kept up the momentum to eliminate Carlito and Chris Masters, leaving Michaels at a 3-to-1 disadvantage. Shawn fought with courage, playing Sweet Chin Music and pinning Rey and JBL back to back, but Randy Orton's RKO overwhelmed him. A venomous Superstar with a standout *Survivor Series* record, Orton defeated Michaels to become the sole survivor (for a third time in his career) and ensure *SmackDown's* supremacy.

FACT

SmackDown reigned over Raw in singles action at Survivor Series 2005 as General Manager Theodore Long defeated Raw General Manager Eric Bischoff.

TEAM SMACKDOWN

SHAWN MICHAELS
STRENGTH

ENDURANCE

KANE
STRENGTH

ENDURANCE

BIG SHOW
STRENGTH

ENDURANCE

CARLITO
STRENGTH

ENDURANCE

CHRIS MASTERS
STRENGTH

ENDURANCE

10 9 8 7 6 5 4 3 2 1

TEAM RAW

2002!
ELIMINATION CHAMBER MATCH FOR THE WORLD HEAVYWEIGHT CHAMPIONSHIP

THE HISTORY

History was made on September 2, 2002, when Eric Bischoff crowned Triple H the first World Heavyweight Champion, bringing a major prize to Raw after the WWE Championship became a SmackDown exclusive. Bischoff's next major game-changer came weeks later with the creation of Elimination Chamber: a 10-ton steel fortress unlike any seen in sports-entertainment. Set to debut at Survivor Series 2002, the Chamber was made for torture and to test the toughness of six Superstars, in this case, all competing for Triple H's title.

VS. VS.

TRIPLE H
SHAWN MICHAELS
CHRIS JERICHO
KANE
BOOKER T
ROB VAN DAM

For months, "The Game" Triple H had crookedly endured challenges by enemies like Rob Van Dam and Kane. Kane nearly beat Triple H in a bout that unified the World Heavyweight and Intercontinental Championships. None of these rivalries was as deep rooted as the one shared between Triple H and ex-best friend-turned-Chamber mate "HBK" Shawn Michaels. HBK's road back to WWE after a career-threatening injury ended in triumph against his former DX partner in an unsanctioned fight at *SummerSlam*. The Game lost to the returning Showstopper but, in a cowardly act, nearly crippled HBK with a targeted sledgehammer strike to his recovering back after the match.

No one expected Michaels to ever set foot inside a ring again, let alone a structure as uncharted and dangerous as the Elimination Chamber. Still, HBK vowed to compete again at *Survivor Series*. If he couldn't win the World Heavyweight Championship, he wanted to ensure that Triple H didn't leave with it in his wicked hands.

THE BATTLE FOR SURVIVAL

The Elimination Chamber's premiere lived up to all the vile expectations of its creator, Eric Bischoff. The domed steel set served as a seventh—and perhaps most dangerous—participant in this contest featuring past and future holders of top titles.

The match kicked off with The Game and RVD, followed by Chris Jericho and Booker T. Early on, the extreme setting appeared mostly to be to RVD's advantage. He used the cage walls to avoid impact as well as mostly high-flying offensive moves, including a Five-Star Frog Splash from the top of a Chamber pod onto Triple H. Van Dam failed to recover from his own landing and Booker's missile dropkick put him away.

FACT

The Elimination Chamber weighs 10 tons and consists of 2 miles (3.2 km) of chain.

Body-crushing collisions with the structure and its pods plus combinations of finishing moves took out Booker. Then Kane received a superkick, Pedigree, and Lionsault before being pinned by Jericho. But Jericho got a dose of Sweet Chin Music while performing the Walls of Jericho on Triple H and was eliminated.

WWE fans continued to believe in HBK as he battled Triple H and kicked out of his enemy's Pedigree. HBK then leveled Triple H with Sweet Chin Music to defeat him, reclaim his first World Championship in four years, and survive the Elimination Chamber.

THE STATS

TRIPLE H
STRENGTH
ENDURANCE

SHAWN MICHAELS
STRENGTH
ENDURANCE

CHRIS JERICHO
STRENGTH
ENDURANCE

KANE
STRENGTH
ENDURANCE

BOOKER T
STRENGTH
ENDURANCE

ROB VAN DAM
STRENGTH
ENDURANCE

10 9 8 7 6 5 4 3 2 1 0

1990: DREAM TEAM VS. MILLION DOLLAR TEAM

THE HISTORY

There was one individual in WWE who took particular exception to "The Million Dollar Man" Ted DiBiase's claim that "everybody had a price." Known as "The American Dream" and "The Common Man," Dusty Rhodes represented the masses. He believed that there was no substitute for hard work. And he was determined to teach Ted DiBiase the most valuable lesson of all at Survivor Series 1990.

To do so, Rhodes enlisted the help of Koko B. Ware and World Tag Team Champions The Hart Foundation, plus the Harts' rivals Rhythm & Blues (Honky Tonky Man and Greg Valentine), and a mystery partner to be revealed live on pay-per-view.

COMBATANTS

DREAM TEAM

DUSTY RHODES (CAPTAIN)

Koko B. Ware

Bret Hart

Jim Neidhart

MILLION DOLLAR TEAM

TED DIBIASE (CAPTAIN)

Undertaker

Honky Tonk Man

Greg Valentine

Months earlier at *SummerSlam*, The Million Dollar Man shocked Rhodes by using the power of money to pay off Dusty's manager, Sapphire. The Million Dollar Man promised yet another "big surprise" for The American Dream at *Survivor Series*. The entire locker room wondered who it might be. But the millionaire's vows to show "no mercy" and claims about leaving Rhodes "begging and humbled" just moments before their showdown wouldn't stop the determined Dusty Rhodes. He and his fellow Dream Team members were prepared to battle and make history against one of the biggest debuts WWE would ever see.

FACT

The Million Dollar Championship was crafted by Betteridge Jewelers in Greenwich, Connecticut, less than 8 miles (12.9 km) from WWE Headquarters.

THE STATS

DUSTY RHODES
STRENGTH

ENDURANCE

KOKO B. WARE
STRENGTH

ENDURANCE

BRET HART
STRENGTH

ENDURANCE

JIM NEIDHART
STRENGTH

ENDURANCE

0 1 2 3 4 5 6 7 8 9 10

THE BATTLE FOR SURVIVAL

No one thought Ted DiBiase would unveil a dark mystery partner from Death Valley. The Million Dollar Team's fourth member was Undertaker, competing in his very first WWE match. His presence would haunt WWE for decades to come.

Before the shock could wear off the WWE fans in attendance, the towering Deadman had already dominated the likes of Bret Hart and Jim Neidhart. He eliminated Koko B. Ware with his maneuver the Tombstone. Undertaker overtook The American Dream next with an impressive top-rope assault unlike any previously seen. The Deadman didn't stop there. He continued to brawl with Dusty Rhodes outside the ring and in the locker room. He was counted out by the official, giving the final member of The Dream Team (Bret Hart) a fighting chance against his last two remaining opponents, DiBiase and Greg Valentine.

DREAM TEAM

Hart managed to defeat and remove Valentine from the bout, but the young Hart couldn't endure the cunning veteran DiBiase. A classic clash of two experts ended with The Million Dollar Man reversing Bret's cross body into a winning pinfall. On this fateful night, DiBiase was the sole survivor, but he shared the spotlight with Bret Hart's breakout moment and the introduction of Undertaker to WWE.

THE STATS

THE MILLION DOLLAR MAN
TED DIBIASE

STRENGTH

ENDURANCE

UNDERTAKER
STRENGTH

ENDURANCE

HONKY TONK MAN
STRENGTH

ENDURANCE

GREG VALENTINE
STRENGTH

ENDURANCE

10 9 8 7 6 5 4 3 2 1 0

FACT

WWE Hall of Famer Koko B. Ware was the first Superstar to ever be Tombstoned by Undertaker.

MILLION DOLLAR TEAM

2001:
TEAM WWE VS. TEAM ALLIANCE

THE HISTORY

In March 2001, WWE Chairman Vince McMahon and son Shane revealed the company's purchase of WCW. McMahon's power play led to what would become known as "The Invasion." That summer former WCW stars suddenly started popping up and interfering in WWE matches.

With a goal of taking over all of sports-entertainment, the rogues of WCW and ECW merged to form The Alliance under the leadership of Stephanie McMahon, Paul Heyman, and Shane himself. The ranks of the rebel group grew as Superstars Kurt Angle and "Stone Cold" Steve Austin (the WWE Champion) betrayed WWE and joined.

||||||||||||||||||||| COMBATANTS |||||||||||||||||||||

TEAM WWE

THE ROCK (CAPTAIN)

Chris Jericho

Undertaker

Kane

Big Show

TEAM ALLIANCE

STONE COLD STEVE AUSTIN (CAPTAIN)

Kurt Angle

Booker T

Rob Van Dam

Shane McMahon

After several months of struggle, Vince McMahon issued a *Survivor Series* challenge to his son and daughter's faction: a "Winner Take All" clash to determine the fates of both forces. The losing side would disband forever.

The Alliance squad included Austin, Angle, Shane O'Mac, Booker T, and Rob Van Dam. WWE's ranks were rounded out by Undertaker, Kane, and The Rock, as well as original WCW defectors Big Show and Chris Jericho. Both sides were strained by trust issues. The ultimate battle for survival would be determined by these ten men in one of the most critical matches ever fought.

FACT

On March 26, 2001, WWE Chairman Vince McMahon and son Shane McMahon appeared on the final episode of WCW Monday Nitro and revealed their purchase of WCW.

THE STATS

THE ROCK
STRENGTH

||||||||||||||||||||||||||||||||||||||||||||

ENDURANCE

||||||||||||||||||||||||||||||||||||||||||||

CHRIS JERICHO
STRENGTH

||||||||||||||||||||||||||||||||||||||

ENDURANCE

||||||||||||||||||||||||||||||||||||||||

UNDERTAKER
STRENGTH

||||||||||||||||||||||||||||||||||||||||||||||

ENDURANCE

||||||||||||||||||||||||||||||||||||||||||||

KANE
STRENGTH

||||||||||||||||||||||||||||||||||||||||||||

ENDURANCE

||||||||||||||||||||||||||||||||||||||||||||

BIG SHOW
STRENGTH

||||||||||||||||||||||||||||||||||||||||||||||||

ENDURANCE

||||||||||||||||||||||||||||||||||||||||||||

0 1 2 3 4 5 6 7 8 9 10

THE BATTLE FOR SURVIVAL

Battle lines were definitely drawn at *Survivor Series* 2001 and the "Winner Take All" collision to decide which organization would thrive. Team WWE's captain The Rock set foot in the ring. The People's Champ quickly blasted the enemies. Defending WWE, The Rock took the fight head-on against The Alliance, and Rock would be his camp's savior.

The defeat of Big Show, Kane, and The Deadman to The Alliance's cheating and underhandedness put WWE's squad at a major disadvantage until Jericho and The Rock set aside their mutual hatred. They rallied back to eliminate Booker T, RVD, and Kurt Angle. Their lead would be short-lived. Austin pinned Jericho, and then the frustrated Y2J attacked his own teammate, The Rock.

FACT

Shane McMahon was the only competitor in this match who has never held a World Championship.

MOVE: THE SHARP SHOOTER

TEAM WWE

After the shocking, cowardly, and traitorous move by Jericho, The Rock fought back with everything he had left. Suddenly, the eliminated Kurt Angle returned to the ring and showed his true colors by blasting Austin with his own WWE Championship!

With Stone Cold rocked by Angle's strike, The Rock scored a pinfall win that stunned a locker room of WCW/ECW competitors, and, more importantly, saved Vince McMahon's company. WWE had survived.

THE STATS

STONE COLD STEVE AUSTIN
STRENGTH

ENDURANCE

KURT ANGLE
STRENGTH

ENDURANCE

BOOKER T
STRENGTH

ENDURANCE

ROB VAN DAM
STRENGTH

ENDURANCE

SHANE MCMAHON
STRENGTH

ENDURANCE

10 9 8 7 6 5 4 3 2 1

TEAM ALLIANCE

APPENDIX: ALL-TIME TOP SURVIVORS

#4: SHAWN MICHAELS

WHY: He may be "Mr. *WrestleMania*," but Shawn Michaels has also stolen the show at *Survivor Series* across three different decades! The WWE Hall of Famer has competed in 17 different *Survivor Series* events, where he captured the WWE Championship from Bret Hart in the most shocking moment in WWE history. He also won his first and only World Heavyweight Championship here in the debut of the Elimination Chamber Match.

SURVIVOR SERIES HISTORY:

1988: **Powers of Pain,** The Rockers, The Young Stallions, The British Bulldogs, and The Hart Foundation def. Demolition, The Rougeau Brothers, The Brainbusters, The Bolsheviks, and Los Conquistadores

1989: **Ultimate Warrior,** The Rockers, and Jim Neidhart def. Andre the Giant, Bobby Heenan, Haku, and Arn Anderson

1990: **Rick Martel, The Warlord,** and Power & Glory def. Jake Roberts, Jimmy Snuka, and The Rockers

1991: **The Nasty Boys, Blake Beverly,** and Beau Beverly def. The Rockers and The Bushwhackers

1992: **Bret Hart** def. Shawn Michaels: WWE Championship Match

1993: **Bret Hart, Keith Hart, Bruce Hart,** and Owen Hart def. Shawn Michaels, The Black Knight, The Red Knight, and The Blue Knight

1994: **Razor Ramon,** 1-2-3 Kid, British Bulldog, and The Headshrinkers def. Shawn Michaels, Diesel, Jeff Jarrett, Owen Hart, and Jim Neidhart

1995: **Shawn Michaels, British Bulldog, Ahmed Johnson,** and Sid def. Razor Ramon, Dean Douglas, Yokozuna, and Owen Hart

1996: **Sid** def. Shawn Michaels: WWE Championship Match

1997: **Shawn Michaels** def. Bret Hart: WWE Championship Match

2002: **Shawn Michaels** def. Triple H, Chris Jericho, Kane, Rob Van Dam, and Booker T: Elimination Chamber Match for the World Heavyweight Championship

2003: **Randy Orton,** Chris Jericho, Christian, Scott Steiner, and Mark Henry def. Shawn Michaels, Rob Van Dam, Booker T, and The Dudley Boyz

2005: **Randy Orton,** Batista, Lashley, Rey Mysterio, and JBL def. Shawn Michaels, Kane, Big Show, Chris Masters, and Carlito

2006: **Triple H, Shawn Michaels, Matt Hardy, Jeff Hardy,** and **CM Punk** def. Edge, Randy Orton, Gregory Helms, Johnny Nitro, and Mike Knox

2007: **Randy Orton** def. Shawn Michaels: WWE Championship Match

2008: **Shawn Michaels, Rey Mysterio, The Great Khali,** and Cryme Tyme def. JBL, MVP, Kane, The Miz, and John Morrison

2009: **John Cena** def. Triple H and Shawn Michaels: Triple Threat Match for the WWE Championship

#3: JOHN CENA

WHY: Since his very first *Survivor Series* in 2003, John Cena has won all but one match he has participated in. He has survived each of his four Traditional Elimination Tag Team Matches, defeating the likes of Brock Lesnar and Big Show, plus, Cena has beaten Triple H, Shawn Michaels, and more in major World Title bouts.

SURVIVOR SERIES HISTORY:

2003: **John Cena** and his team def. Brock Lesnar, Big Show, Albert, Nathan Jones, and Matt Morgan

2004: **John Cena, Eddie Guerrero, Big Show,** and Rob Van Dam def. Kurt Angle, Carlito, Luther Reigns, and Mark Jindrak

2005: **John Cena** def. Kurt Angle: WWE Championship Match

2006: **John Cena,** Lashley, Kane, Rob Van Dam, and Sabu def. Big Show, Finlay, Test, MVP, and Umaga

2008: **John Cena** def. Chris Jericho: World Heavyweight Championship Match

2009: **John Cena** def. Triple H and Shawn Michaels: Triple Threat Match for the WWE Championship

2011: **John Cena** and **The Rock** def. The Miz and R-Truth

2012: **CM Punk** def. John Cena and Ryback: Triple Threat Match for the WWE Championship

2013: **John Cena** def. Alberto Del Rio: World Heavyweight Championship Match

#2: RANDY ORTON

WHY: Like the snake he's nicknamed after, The Viper has the will to survive. Randy Orton was the sole survivor in three straight Traditional Elimination Tag Team Matches (2003, 2004, and 2005), which no other Superstar in history had ever done before. On top of his tag-team mastery, Orton has also RKO'd his way to victory in multiple WWE Championship bouts at *Survivor Series*.

SURVIVOR SERIES HISTORY:

2003: **Randy Orton,** Chris Jericho, Christian, Scott Steiner, and Mark Henry def. Shawn Michaels, Rob Van Dam, Booker T, and The Dudley Boyz

2004: **Randy Orton** and his team def. Triple H, Batista, Snitsky, and Edge

2005: **Randy Orton,** Batista, Lashley, Rey Mysterio, and JBL def. Shawn Michaels, Kane, Big Show, Chris Masters, and Carlito

2006: **Triple H, Shawn Michaels, Matt Hardy, Jeff Hardy,** and **CM Punk** def. Edge, Randy Orton, Gregory Helms, Johnny Nitro, and Mike Knox

2007: **Randy Orton** def. Shawn Michaels: WWE Championship Match

2008: **Randy Orton, Cody Rhodes,** Shelton Benjamin, Mark Henry, and William Regal def. Batista, CM Punk, Kofi Kingston, Matt Hardy, and R-Truth

2009: **Kofi Kingston,** R-Truth, MVP, Christian, and Mark Henry def. Randy Orton, Ted DiBiase, Cody Rhodes, William Regal, and CM Punk

2010: **Randy Orton** def. Wade Barrett: WWE Championship Match w/ special referee John Cena

2011: **Wade Barrett, Cody Rhodes,** Dolph Ziggler, Jack Swagger, and Hunico def. Randy Orton, Sheamus, Kofi Kingston, Mason Ryan, and Sin Cara

2012: **Dolph Ziggler,** Wade Barrett, Alberto Del Rio, David Otunga, and Damien Sandow def. Randy Orton, The Miz, Kofi Kingston, Kane, and Daniel Bryan

2013: **Randy Orton** def. Big Show: WWE Championship Match

#1: UNDERTAKER

WHY: Ever since he made his chilling WWE debut in 1990, Undertaker has used *Survivor Series* as his stage for vengeance. He has made many major returns to action at the November classic, where he has competed in everything from a Buried Alive Match to a Hell in a Cell Match. The Deadman captured his first-ever title at *Survivor Series* 1991 by defeating WWE Champion Hulk Hogan. He helped save WWE in 2001 against The Alliance. Plus, he has dominated WWE's giants in three different Casket Matches—a contest he introduced at this event. There's no questioning that *Survivor Series* belongs to Undertaker.

SURVIVOR SERIES HISTORY:

1990: **Ted DiBiase,** Undertaker, Honky Tonk Man, and Greg Valentine def. Dusty Rhodes, Bret Hart, Jim Neidhart, and Koko B. Ware

1991: **Undertaker** def. Hulk Hogan: WWE Championship Match

1992: **Undertaker** def. Kamala: Casket Match

1993: **Lex Luger,** Undertaker, and The Steiner Brothers def. Yokozuna, Ludvig Borga, Crush, and Quebecer Jacques

1994: **Undertaker** def. Yokozuna: Casket Match

1995: **Undertaker, Savio Vega, Henry O. Godwinn,** and Fatu def. King Mabel, Jerry Lawler, Hunter Hearst-Helmsley, and Isaac Yankem

1996: **Undertaker** def. Mankind

1998: **Undertaker** def. Kane; **The Rock** def. Undertaker: WWE Championship Tournament

2000: **Kurt Angle** def. Undertaker: WWE Championship Match

2001: **The Rock,** Undertaker, Chris Jericho, Kane, and Big Show def. Stone Cold Steve Austin, Kurt Angle, Shane McMahon, Booker T, and Rob Van Dam

2003: **Mr. McMahon** def. Undertaker: Buried Alive Match

2004: **Undertaker** def. Heidenreich

2006: **Mr. Kennedy** def. Undertaker: First Blood Match

2007: **Batista** def. Undertaker: Hell in a Cell World Heavyweight Championship Match

2008: **Undertaker** def. Big Show: Casket Match

2009: **Undertaker** def. Big Show and Chris Jericho: Triple Threat Match for the World Heavyweight Championship